Preventing Office Staff Fraud

Preventing Office Staff Fraud

A practical guide for physicians, business owners, and office leaders to prevent, deter, and detect employee fraud—including embezzlement.

S. Gerard Ruby, MD, MBA

1st Edition, May 1, 2026

Published by Ruby Group Ltd.
PO Box 331
Fortville, Indiana 46040
USA

inquiry@rubygrouppublishing.com

ISBN: 978-0-9896911-3-0

Copyright and Disclaimer

The information and content provided in this book are for general information purposes only. This book has been produced on a best-effort basis. The author and publisher have made every effort to ensure the accuracy of the information presented herein, but do not guarantee or warranty completeness, adequacy or currency of the content. Readers should consult with appropriate professionals or experts in specific areas if they require personalized advice or assistance. This publication does not constitute legal, accounting, financial, or employment advice. Laws and regulations vary by jurisdiction, and readers are responsible for ensuring compliance with applicable laws.

You are recommended to consult with your local professionals as relevant to your circumstances and legal jurisdiction.

The author and publisher shall have no liability for any loss, injury, or damages from the use or reliance on the information contained in this book. They disclaim all responsibility for any errors or omissions in the content. Additionally, the author and publisher do not assume any responsibility or liability for third-party content linked to or referenced in this book. You alone are responsible for any actions you take, fail to take or choose to not to take.

Any resemblance to actual persons, living or dead, or events is purely coincidental.

By reading this book, you acknowledge and agree to the terms of the disclaimer. If you do not agree with these terms, you should not read this book.

Visit **www.RubyGroupPublishing.com** for supplemental materials, practical worksheets, and additional resources.

Also by the Author

Monarchy to Democracy: The Most Dangerous Transition in Business Ownership

Available on Amazon

Ruby Group Ltd. (2026)

What others say about business fraud...

"The most common fraudster is a first-time offender."

"Fraud is rarely detected by accident; it is discovered through tips and active monitoring."

— Association of Certified Fraud Examiners (ACFE), Report to the Nations

"The opportunity to commit fraud is the element that organizations can most directly affect through internal controls."

— Joseph T. Wells, Corporate Fraud Handbook

"Good internal controls do not eliminate fraud — they reduce opportunity and increase detection."

— COSO Framework

"Internal control is a process, effected by an entity's board of directors, management, and other personnel."

— Committee of Sponsoring Organizations of the Treadway Commission (COSO)

Table of Contents

Introduction

Physician practices don't fail because doctors forget medicine. They fail because no one is watching the money closely enough.

Fraud rarely begins with a single event. It develops quietly—through small gaps, routine habits, and systems no one questions. By the time it's discovered, the damage is already done.

At first, the pressure doesn't feel like fraud. It feels administrative—small issues that are easy to overlook until they aren't. Cash leakage, fake invoices, payroll padding, unexplained write-offs, stolen supplies, or missing deposits. Over time, these add up to something far more serious: the slow erosion of trust.

Office staff fraud is especially damaging because it hits in two places at once—your finances and your bandwidth. It shows up as meetings, audits, attorney calls, staff tension, and the question that follows every discovery:

What else did we miss?

This isn't something that just large organizations need to consider. I have personally encountered two cases of fraud in small physician offices over a ten-year period—and those are only the ones that were discovered. I have also experienced smaller fraudulent activity in my own practice, including payroll padding and petty theft of supplies. No business is immune.

The hardest truth is also the most freeing one: you can't make fraud impossible. Any clever person with enough access can do damage. In fact, according to the Association of Certified Fraud Examiners' 2024 Report to the Nations, the median loss from occupational fraud is $117,000. Small organizations with fewer than 100 employees actually suffer disproportionately higher median losses despite having fewer transactions. The healthcare sector sees fraud that lasts a median of 18 months before detection—enough time for losses to compound significantly.

But you can make fraud harder, riskier, and more likely to be detected early. The more likely detection is in a practice, the less likely someone is to attempt fraudulent activity. More than 30% of fraudulent activity is associated with inadequate internal controls or overrides of those controls. And good systems for internal detection work. It has been reported that more than 40% of fraud is detected by tips from employees, customers, or vendors. Takeaway: Listen to people. Have a non-retaliation statement in your employee handbook to help people feel safer about reporting fraudulent activity.

This booklet focuses on practical habits—many suitable for handbooks and onboarding—that make fraud harder to commit and easier to detect. It provides useful tips and easy suggestions, but the most important tip is this: Do something. None of these elements will work if you don't take action!

If you think fraud can't happen in your business, that belief is a serious risk factor. This book is intended to help you eliminate that risk factor - first.

This book is written for individuals responsible for the oversight and protection of financial and operational assets—including business owners, physician leaders, office managers, and anyone involved in fraud detection and prevention.

Five Common Beliefs That Cost Business Owners Thousands

It doesn't matter what type of business you run — a medical practice, legal office, accounting firm, or professional service. Across industries, owners repeat the same beliefs about fraud. These "beliefs" are understandable. They are common. But they are expensive.

Below are five beliefs most business owners hold — and why they are wrong.

Belief #1: "My staff wouldn't do that."

Most internal fraud is committed by trusted, long-term employees — not strangers. Trust is not a control system. According to the ACFE, fraudsters with more than 10 years of tenure at their organization cause median losses of $200,000—nearly double the overall median. The longer someone has been with you, the more access and knowledge they have, and the more damage they can do, if tempted.

Belief #2: "I'd notice if something was wrong."

Fraud rarely appears as a single alarming event. It emerges gradually through small, rationalized actions hidden in routine transactions. The ACFE reports that occupational fraud lasts a median of 12 months before detection—18 months in healthcare settings. If you don't look, you don't find. And even when you look, you need to know what you're looking for. And if you find it, don't ignore it.

Belief #3: "We're too small to be a target."

Small practices are easier targets, not harder ones. Organizations with fewer than 100 employees suffer disproportionately higher median losses ($150,000) compared to larger organizations. Why? Controls are informal, oversight is predictable, one person often handles transactions end-to-end, and there's an assumption that "everyone knows everyone" so fraud won't happen.

Belief #4: "Software and accountants would catch it."

Tools and reports only detect fraud if someone reviews them, understands them, and acts on what they see. Accounting software doesn't prevent fake vendors. Your bookkeeper can override controls. Your accountant only sees what you show them. Technology is a tool, not a solution. According to industry data, fewer than 15% of frauds are detected by external audits—most are caught by tips or internal controls actually being used.

Belief #5: "Dealing with fraud would destroy morale."

In reality, clear controls and fair enforcement protect honest employees and increase trust — silence and avoidance do the opposite. Honest staff appreciate knowing the rules are real and apply to everyone. What destroys morale is selective enforcement, ignored violations, and the creeping suspicion that someone is getting away with something while everyone else follows the rules.

Bottom line:

Fraud rarely starts with bad intent. It requires opportunity, routine, and a lack of consistent oversight. I call it the "Fraud Triangle": Pressure + Opportunity + Rationalization. Reduce any of those elements and you can reduce the chance of fraud. Prevention isn't about suspicion—it's about structure, detection and action.

The Habit Advantage: Consistency Beats Intensity

Why steady oversight outperforms dramatic intervention

It had never been one big lapse. It was dozens of small ones. A skipped review here. A postponed reconciliation there. Everyone meant well. The practice was busy.

Then the owner began doing something different. Not dramatic. Just consistent. Every Friday, there was the same review. Every month, the same financial check.

But that wasn't all. A small check on operations—randomly and unpredictably, became the new norm.

Nothing felt heavy-handed. The controls that were put into place were those that any responsible business would have.

But the new oversight was clear: the risk of fraud being detected had quietly increased. Visibly, to all employees.

The staff noticed these small changes. Staff behavior changed because the risk of detection had increased.

*****

Fraud hides in routine. Regular review turns routine activity into something you can actually see. Commonly, "things tighten up" after a scare, then drift back to comfort. Staff learns the pattern. A dishonest employee learns it faster.

What works is not a sweeping crackdown. It's visible, repeatable habits that say—every day—"This practice is watched."

Think of fraud prevention like hygiene. You don't brush your teeth once a month and call it discipline. You build a short routine that's easy to sustain. In a practice, that routine is a set of small actions: a quick review of daily totals, a random glance at receipt sequences, a monthly owner review of bank activity, and a surprise audit of something small.

Most employees will never steal. That's good. These habits aren't about fear. They're about clarity. When oversight is steady, opportunity shrinks. When oversight is unpredictable, temptation weakens. When oversight is normal and not reactive, your staff sees it as professionalism—not mistrust.

Your goal stays constant: prevent, deter, and detect.

Key Principle: Fraud prevention works when oversight is consistent, visible, and unpredictable — not intense and short-lived.

Preventative Habits To Start

Pick three controls you will do weekly, and schedule them like patient appointments. Some common detection methods (in addition to tips from employees, vendors and customers) include audits (self and external) or management reviews. Some of these will be covered in the next chapters.

Make one control random (day/time changes).

Make one control visible (staff should know you review it).

Notes

What habits do you already have to help reduce fraud? What habits can you think of ...right now, that you know you could easily implement? It doesn't have to be hard or complex, just visible.

The Fraud Triangle: Pressure + Opportunity + Rationalization

How opportunity turns stress into theft

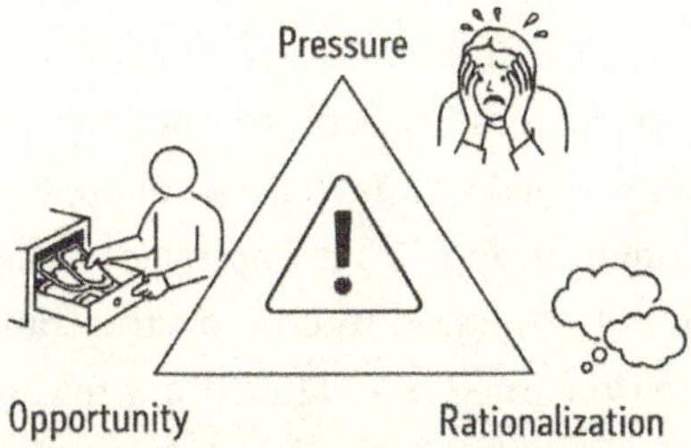

Bills had piled up at home. He knew exactly how financial adjustments were entered at work—and who never checked them.

Those adjustments had always seemed predictable. An easy opportunity. Until recently.

The process itself hadn't changed much. But the oversight had. Adjustments were now reviewed. Sometimes immediately. Sometimes later. Never the same way twice.

The pressure of the home bills was still there.

But the opportunity of an easy financial "help" from the practice no longer was. It simply wasn't worth the new risk.

*****

Fraud usually isn't born from evil. It starts with personal financial **pressure**. It's born from a moment when someone decides they "deserve" something—and the **opportunity** where they believe they can take it without consequences. They **rationalize** theft as temporary relief from personal pressure, then convince themselves it will go unnoticed. Most fraud is internal and by people who know the business well, such as your employees. The higher up they are in management, the greater the potential for fraud loss.

Pressure can be financial stress, addiction, gambling, divorce, medical bills, or resentment. Opportunity is the open door: one person handling money end-to-end, weak receipts, loose refunds, unquestioned write-offs, and deposits no one verifies. Rationalization is how employees considering fraud give themselves permission to commit the fraud. "You deserve it." "You earned it." "They don't reward you enough."

Together, Pressure, Opportunity, and Rationalization comprise the "Fraud Triangle."

You can't control someone's private life. But you can control opportunity. Pressure creates motive. Opportunity creates action. Rationalization provides permission. Remove opportunity, and most fraud never starts. Not every discrepancy is fraud, but discrepancies that go undetected are often the root cause of fraud. Effective controls can weaken one or more of the legs of the Fraud Triangle in your business.

Key Principle: Pressure + Opportunity = Risk. You can only control opportunity. It's your job to remove that Fraud Triangle "leg."

Preventative Habits To Start

Identify the top 3 access points: For example, cash, refunds/write-offs, vendor payments.

For each, remove "one-person start-to-finish" control.

Add one independent visible verification step staff can't predict.

Notes

Do you see any of these risk factors in your current employees? How can you become more aware of them in your business? What systems are unmonitored by you?

Know the Playing Field: Common Fraud Types

The fraud patterns every practice should recognize

The owner couldn't explain why refunds were creeping up. No single one stood out. But together, they didn't make sense.

It was time to get to the bottom of it. Was it honest? Or something else?

Once the categories were separated—refunds, write-offs, supply losses—the pattern emerged. And it didn't make sense until someone categorized the transactions and reviewed them. Then the opportunity, and the fix became obvious.

It wasn't sophisticated fraud. It was someone taking advantage of a simple situation that could easily be missed.

Only now, it didn't go undetected. It was being reviewed and managed. Visibly.

*****

Most practice fraud fits into recognizable buckets: skimming, cash theft, asset theft, payroll fraud, and expense fraud. The value of naming these isn't academic—it gives you a map to better understand the specific risk areas in your business. When transactions are grouped and reviewed, irregularities stop blending in. They stand out.

Owners often overbuild controls in the wrong places, or incompletely: locking down supply closets while refunds remain wide open or obsessing over petty cash while vendor payments run on autopilot. Asset misappropriation is the most common type of fraud, around 90% of reported fraudulent activity. But it's not just money. Theft can involve inventory, supplies and, in medical settings, pharmaceuticals. Those types of fraud may have special reporting requirements that you should be aware of. Pharmaceutical theft in particular carries mandatory federal reporting obligations under DEA regulations—including DEA Form 106 for theft or significant loss of controlled substances. (See Chapter 17 for the response framework and the Useful References section at the back of this book for direct links to DEA reporting resources.)

Other types of fraud that occur include corruption, including kickbacks (for instance, in conjunction with vendors) or accepting bribes. Financial statement fraud isn't as common, but if it occurs, it can be very costly. And don't forget about billing fraud which might be difficult to catch because of the complexity, especially in medical offices. The opportunities are many.

Technology-specific fraud risks are growing

New fraud opportunities emerge with technology: telemedicine billing fraud (billing for services not rendered or upcoding virtual visits), EHR manipulation (altering records to support fraudulent billing or hide theft), electronic prescription fraud (diverting controlled substances), and remote work vulnerabilities (reduced oversight when staff work from home). These require specific monitoring beyond traditional controls.

Match the control to the risk: high-frequency money touchpoints get daily/weekly habits; lower-frequency but high-dollar processes get monthly review. Ultra-high risk items, such as medications and drugs warrant constant surveillance.

It's also important to consider fraud that may occur in any of your outsourced financial activities. Schedule an appointment with your vendors for the explicit discussion of their fraud risk prevention activities and policies.

Key Principle: Fraud becomes visible when transactions are categorized and reviewed, not guessed.

Preventative Habits To Start

Write down where money enters/leaves your practice in 10 lines.

Circle the three opportunities where one person can act alone.

Start controls there first.

Notes

What fraud types are easiest in your office? Which are "hidden" from you that you should be aware of? Which preventative actions can you start immediately?

Hire and Onboard Prevention

Setting expectations before problems begin

Setting Expectations

During orientation, the new hire skimmed the handbook section on financial controls.

It was clear. Direct. Calmly written. Fraud detection activities of the business.

Later, she said, "I appreciate that this is spelled out."

The practice didn't just hire for skills. It lived up to expectations.

The potential "bad actors" self-selected to not apply any longer.

*****

Hiring is your first fraud control because it sets expectations. Honest people don't fear honest screening or monitoring.

Make integrity part of the practice brand: "We run a tight ship." "We audit randomly." "We separate duties on money."

Then reinforce it during onboarding and in the employee handbook: money-handling standards, refund rules, receipt rules, and the reporting path belong in writing—not just verbal tradition.

A handbook doesn't prevent fraud by itself. But it removes ambiguity, strengthens enforcement, and supports consistent training.

Key Principle: Hiring and onboarding set expectations that deter fraud before it starts.

Preventative Habits To Start

Add a one-page "Money Handling Standards" handout to onboarding and include it in the handbook.

Have staff sign acknowledgement annually (not just at hire).

State clearly: random audits occur.

Notes

Do you have questions and/or policies that will help current and future prospects "self-select" to not continue looking for employment with you?

Assign Roles, Not People

Segregation of duties in real-world offices

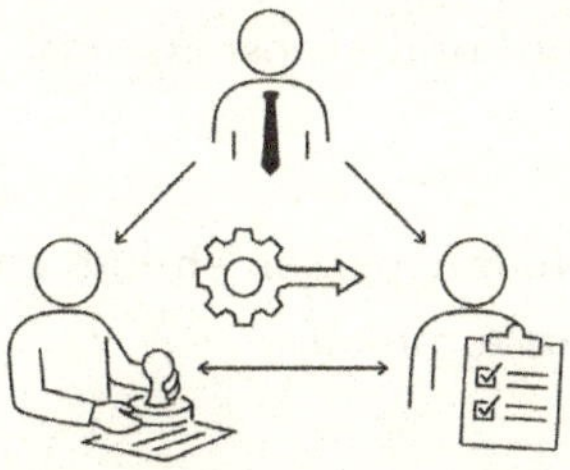

Segregation of Duties

For years, one person handled deposits start to finish. It was efficient. Trusted. Easy. Perhaps too easy.

When roles were split, the work barely changed. No one complained.

But something else did: accountability was now an integral component of the system.

And it worked.

*****

Most embezzlement becomes possible when a person can create, approve, and reconcile the same financial transaction stream.

For a small practice, you don't need a big corporate structure. You need a two-sets-of-eyes rule on the pathways most often abused: collecting payments, posting payments, refunds and adjustments, deposits, vendor additions, and vendor payments.

Even with a small staff, splitting steps is possible—especially if the owner does the review role.

Everyone in your business should have defined roles to help reduce the Fraud Triangle. You too, as business owner, are part of that. It is one of the most essential roles that you need to embrace.

Key Principle: No one person should control a financial process from start to finish.

Preventative Habits To Start

No one person should receive + post + reconcile.

Owner reviews refunds/adjustments weekly.

Owner reviews deposit totals against daily reports.

Notes

What practices in your business are handled solely by one individual? How can you change that to ensure more accountability?

Small Infractions are Like Smoke

Why ignoring small violations invites larger ones

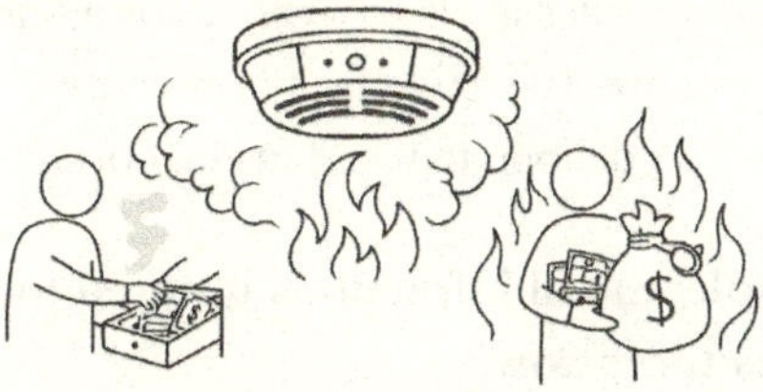

Smoke Signals

It was just a missing receipt. No big deal.

Except it happened again. And this time, the manager detected it and documented it. Briefly. Calmly.

The behavior stopped—not because of fear, but because there was detection, and the rules were real again.

*****

Small infractions that slide become permission for bigger ones. When the owner avoids a minor confrontation, the wrong person reads it as weakness.

Responding doesn't require anger. It requires documentation and clarity: this is the policy, this is the expectation, this is documented, and this is what happens next time.

Your goal is not punishment. It's to remove ambiguity.

Controls, Documentation, and Discipline: Three Distinct Functions

Controls reduce and limit opportunity.

Documentation protects the practice and the owner.

Discipline enforces accountability and boundaries.

Confusing these roles leads to overreaction, inconsistency, and legal exposure. Effective fraud prevention requires all three — applied deliberately and in the correct order.

Key Principle: Small infractions ignored today become large losses tomorrow.

Preventative Habits To Start

Document minor issues in writing (brief, factual, dated).

Make consequences known in advance (handbook + reminders).

Review one "small control" publicly each month.

Notes

Do you let small infractions "go"? If so why? How can you establish a system that deals with these small infractions appropriately?

Money Trail: Trends, Reports, & "What Changed?"

Using trends to spot trouble early

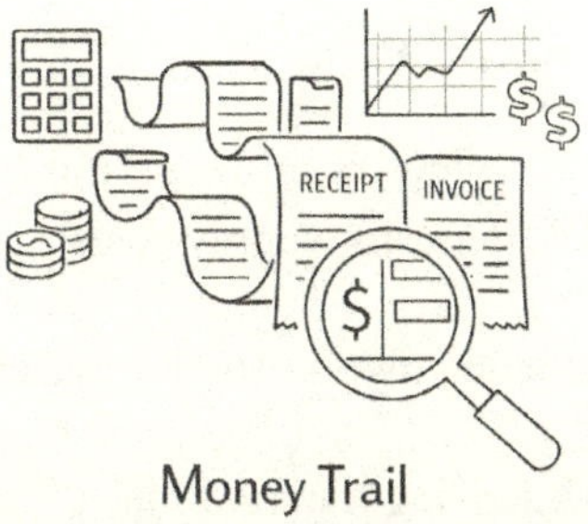

The numbers weren't alarming. Just… different.

Refunds were up. Visits were flat.

When asked to explain the change, the explanation came quickly—and a bit too defensively. That told the owner everything he needed to know.

It was past time for the financial systems to be tightened up.

*****

Fraud hides in noise. Your best weapon is pattern recognition, not suspicion.

Adopt a simple owner habit: "What changed this month?" "Does that change make sense?" "If not, show me the trail."

Examples worth watching: A/R drops while visits rise; refunds rise without explanation; write-offs drift upward; supply costs increase without volume change.

You're not looking for perfection. You're looking for movement.

Key Principle: Fraud reveals itself through changes, not totals.

Preventative Habits To Start

Pick 5 metrics and review monthly (example: A/R aging, refunds, write-offs, deposits, supply costs).

Require written documentation for anomalies.

Spot-check the underlying transactions.

Notes

Do you pay attention to month-to-month changes? Trends? Exceptions? If not, what can you do to initiate this process in your business to help identify such trends earlier?

Receipts, Numbers, and Front-Desk Controls

Simple solutions to spot trouble early

Front Office Transaction Control

The sign had been there for two years. Please request your receipt.

Most patients did. Some didn't notice. For a while, neither did anyone else.

When a routine reconciliation finally happened, three gaps showed up in the receipt sequence over six weeks. Small amounts. Explainable, maybe.

But there was no explanation. Just the gaps.

What followed wasn't dramatic. A new receipt policy. A daily count. The sign now meant something because someone actually checked as an element of the policy.

The gaps stopped. What had happened in those six weeks was never confirmed.

That was the lesson. It was learned by all.

*****

Front-desk cash handling doesn't need to be complex. It just needs to be auditable.

Provide receipts for every transaction and encourage patients to expect them. Use systems that limit voids/changes and rely on sequentially numbered receipts so missing numbers stand out.

Two guardrails reduce abuse: no cash refunds (refund to original method only), and owner approval over a threshold for refunds/adjustments.

An often-overlooked area in a physician office is Electronic Health Record (EHR) access. Such access, when inappropriate, may be a source of nefarious activity. Periodic reviews of EHR activity are warranted to detect such inappropriate access to patient records.

Key Principle: Every transaction should leave a visible, auditable trail.

Preventative Habits To Start

Post a small sign: "Receipts provided for all transactions."

Review receipt sequences randomly.

Set and enforce a refund rule (method + approval threshold).

Notes

What front-end controls, policies and procedures do you have to create accountability? What could you easily implement to achieve such accountability?

Open the Mail, Control the Deposits

Preventing skimming before it starts

Mail Control

Checks used to pass through only one set of hands before the bank. But it became clear that process was a source of opportunity that needed to be changed.

Now the owner saw them first. There was a simple daily count of the number of deposits. It was matched up with the deposit slip.

Nothing else changed—except that having a check "go missing" stopped being easy.

*****

Check skimming is fast and easy to hide unless the owner controls intake. That's why it can commonly occur.

Simple changes - Owner mail review (or a PO box / lockbox), quick copying/scanning of checks, and ensuring deposits match daily reports all reduce opportunity.

The theme is simple: no invisible money.

Key Principle: Money that passes unseen is money that can disappear.

Preventative Habits To Start

Owner reviews incoming payments before posting.

Daily deposit totals and numbers match daily reports.

Deposit quickly—delay creates opportunity and excuses.

Notes

Who controls the deposits? Who controls the money? How is the mail, with payments, handled in your business? Can there be diversion? Who signs the checks? If it's not you, why not? What will you change?

Bank Controls

Using banks as partners in fraud detection

Banking Security

The bank called about a flagged payment.

Casually, the doctor mentioned it at the front desk in conversation.

It turned out to be legitimate. But the message was clear: the system was watching too. There were no hidden actions.

That alone prevented any future attempt one may have thought about.

*****

As the owner, establish these essential processes: limit access to checks, restrict check signers, secure blank checks, and require invoice attachment for every check. See if your banking institution or other financial vendors have the ability, have them provide you with regular access logs for review.

You can further strengthen these policies with modern bank tools: Positive Pay, ACH filters/blocks, dual approval for outgoing electronic payments, and real-time alerts for large withdrawals or new payees.

These controls don't replace owner oversight. They reinforce it.

Remember: Automation helps, but it doesn't stop fraud by itself. Reports only matter if someone reads them and acts on them. Software cannot replace oversight; it only supports it. Reports reviewed late often mean fraud is discovered late.

Key Principle: Bank tools reinforce oversight but never replace it.

Preventative Habits To Start

Reduce check signers to the minimum.

Require invoice attachment for every check.

Ask your bank about Positive Pay + ACH controls.

Notes

Is your bank your partner in fraud reduction? If not, can you talk with your banker to see what types of services they can provide to help you better secure your money?

The Power of Random Audits

Why unpredictability changes behavior

Random Audits

The audit didn't catch anything nefarious.

But everyone knew it could have.

That was enough. It caught the attention of the office staff.

That awareness alone was sufficient to make a difference.

*****

Randomness is a fraud deterrent because it attacks confidence. When oversight is predictable, the dishonest person works around it.

Do frequent small audits rather than just a rare comprehensive audit: random receipt sequence checks, spot-checks of adjustments, random review of deposits and refunds.

Even the announced possibility of a "mystery patient" visit can reduce skimming risk—because staff cannot predict when transactions will be verified.

Some types of audits that can be done (scheduled, random, secret and public) include review of financial statements, budget comparisons and analytics for outliers and regular inventory assessments.

Key Principle: Unpredictable review is one of the strongest fraud deterrents.

Preventative Habits To Start

Create a 12-month audit checklist with random dates, as a reminder for yourself. Don't announce these dates.

Announce that random verification occurs.

Do small audits often.

Notes

Are you too predictable? What can you do to create a degree of unpredictability in your business?

Watch For Human Signals

Managing risk without confronting employees

Warning Signs

She never took a vacation. She always volunteered to stay late. She never asked for help.

For years, those things felt like loyalty. Like dedication. That's how they were treated.

Then a backup was trained—not out of suspicion, but because the practice needed redundancy. The resistance was immediate. Uncomfortable in a way that was hard to name.

The owner didn't address the resistance directly. Just kept going—backup coverage, rotation, a second set of eyes on accounts that had always been managed alone.

The discomfort lasted a few weeks. Then something shifted. Whether that shift was relief, recalibration, or something else was never entirely clear.

The controls stayed. So did she—for a while.

*****

Some behaviors correlate with higher fraud risk: never taking a vacation, odd hours alone in the office, possessiveness over duties, refusal to cross-train, and resistance to controls.

These behaviors are not proof of wrongdoing. They are reasons to tighten controls and highlight areas where controls should be strengthened.

Life stressors—substance abuse, gambling, major debt—can increase temptation. These are one of the legs of the Fraud Triangle: Pressure. The presence of this leg should not be considered guilt. The presence of these issues are signals to tighten controls around the role, not to shame the person. The major point is that it is far easier, less costly, less disruptive, and less stressful to prevent fraud than it is to detect and remediate it.

Some areas to focus on: ensuring systems have controls, such as approvals for large purchases, refunds or override of those controls; lack of audits or reporting systems; and lack of close oversight of all, even trusted, employees.

The correct response to such behavior is structured: mandatory vacation, cross-training, and more than one person touching every financial process.

Red Flags by Role

Different positions show different warning signs:

Billing staff: Increased adjustments without explanation, defensive about accounts receivable aging, resists dual review of refunds.

Front desk: Missing receipt numbers, reluctance to provide receipts to patients, cash drawer variances.

Office manager: Resists vacation, controls all vendor relationships, defensive about financial reports.

Bookkeeper: Lives beyond apparent means, unusually close vendor relationships, resists sharing system access.

Key Principle: Behavioral warning signs call for more attention and stronger process controls.

Preventative Habits To Start

Require vacations for money-handling roles.

Cross-train at least one backup for every financial function.

Increase review cadence when risk signals appear.

Notes

Do you have employees who are too dedicated? That make them feel "indispensable"? Those who refuse to share jobs? Or refuse to take time off?

Payroll Fraud: Time Theft

Preventing work hour theft - on automatic

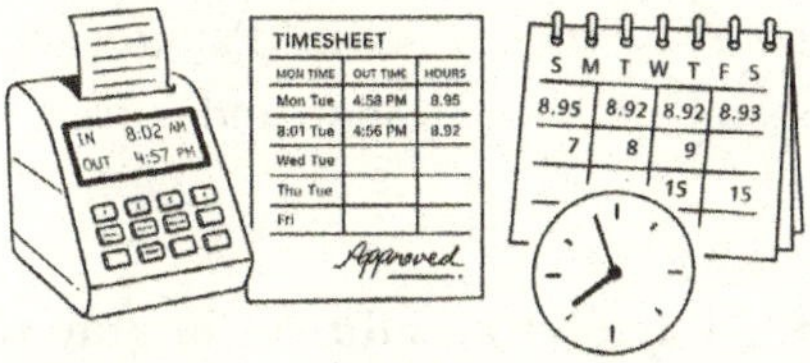

Time Tracking and Payroll Control

Time edits were rare. Until they weren't.

Once edits required approval, the pattern disappeared.

An improved time system didn't hurt either.

No employee confrontation needed.

*****

Time fraud is common because it feels harmless to the person doing it. In the aggregate, it's expensive. A five-minute "pad" each day equals more than 20 hours per year. That can get expensive.

Make payroll fair and clean: one timekeeping method for everyone, defined overtime approval, manager approval for edits, and monthly audits of exceptions (edits, late punches, repeated rounding numbers). Also, outline in your personnel manual that payroll time padding or punching in/out other people is a form of fraud and theft. Remedial actions should follow applicable law and documented policy. Having it known, and in your handbook, can go a long way to preventing it and help defend against it. It's the intentional action and misrepresentation or concealment that represents actionable misconduct, not the isolated error.

You're not trying to catch everyone. You're removing the gray zone where "everyone does it." Patterns indicate risk; isolated errors require investigation and correction, not accusation.

Key Principle: Payroll fraud thrives in gray zones. It's your responsibility to eliminate the gray.

Preventative Habits To Start

Require pre-approval for overtime in writing.

Audit time edits monthly.

Investigate patterns, not one-offs.

Notes

How is payroll managed? Who has access to documentation of and payment for hours worked? Do the hours worked match the work performed? Do you monitor this? Do you have an overtime policy?

Vendor Fraud and Supply Leakage

Closing the gaps that vendors and employees can exploit

Vendor Fraud

The invoice matched the payment. The payment matched the ledger.

But the delivery never arrived.

The vendor said it was a shipping error. A credit was issued. The matter was closed.

Except a review of the prior six months turned up two similar instances. Each one had an explanation. Each explanation was plausible. None could be disproven.

The vendor relationship continued. The staff didn't change. But the verification process did.

Now every delivery gets confirmed before the invoice is approved. Not because anything nefarious was proven. Because something didn't add up—and that was enough.

*****

Friendly vendors are great. But cordiality doesn't guarantee honesty. Strict controls do.

Vendor fraud often looks like padded invoices, absent deliveries, fake companies, or "helpful" ordering that quietly benefits an employee.

Match shipment to invoice and invoice to payment. Control the vendor master list so only owners/managers can add or modify vendors. Review credit memos and returns—common hiding spots.

Reduce quiet theft with periodic inventory spot checks and tighter controls on high-value or regulated items.

Key Principle: Vendor fraud hides where verification is assumed instead of required.

Preventative Habits To Start

Match packing slip → invoice → payment every time.

Restrict vendor creation/edit rights.

Spot-check inventory monthly.

Notes

How well do you monitor the entire vendor process? From orders, to payments to deliveries? Could you identify a source of "padding"?

Corporate Culture: Handbook Reinforcement

Making honesty safe and expected

Positive Culture

The internal office reporting email sat unused for months.

Then one message came in. Quiet. Factual.

The issue was small—and addressed quickly.

The reporting employee was privately thanked.

The owners didn't make a general announcement. They didn't need to.

Trust increased, not decreased.

*****

Culture is not defined by a motivational poster. Culture is what gets reviewed, documented, rewarded, and corrected.

If you want honesty, make honesty safe: publish a confidential reporting path, include a non-retaliation statement, and act on proven facts.

If you want consistency, put the key controls into your employee handbook and onboarding: money-handling standards, refund rules, reporting, audit expectations, and the consequences for intentional theft.

A handbook doesn't replace oversight. But it supports training, reduces disputes, and strengthens your position if discipline or termination becomes necessary.

Key Principle: Culture is created by what is documented, reviewed, and enforced.

Preventative Habits To Start

Publish a confidential reporting path to owners (handbook + onboarding).

Review and refresh fraud policy annually.

Reward one staff improvement regularly.

Notes

Does your handbook have policies and procedures that clearly spell out your expectations regarding employee honesty? Does it have a clearly defined process when such dishonesty is found? It's better to have this done up front, than after the fact.

Insurance: Your Financial Backstop

When prevention isn't enough

Insurance Protection

She'd done everything right. Separated duties. Required approvals. Reviewed monthly reports.

And yet, over eighteen months, a trusted bookkeeper had created fake vendor accounts and siphoned off $73,000.

The discovery was painful. The investigation was expensive. The legal fees mounted.

But the practice had employee dishonesty coverage. The insurer covered most of the loss—because the owner had documented controls, reported promptly, and preserved evidence.

The insurance didn't prevent the fraud. But it prevented financial ruin.

*****

Fraud prevention is your first line of defense. Insurance is your second. Even with strong controls, a determined employee will find a way around them. Insurance is what keeps a bad situation from becoming a financially catastrophic one.

Most practice owners don't think seriously about fraud insurance until they need it. By then, it's too late. The time to understand your coverage is before fraud happens—not after.

Three Types of Coverage to Know

There are three types of insurance relevant to internal fraud. You don't necessarily need all three, but you need to know what each one does so you can decide the desired coverage.

Employee Dishonesty Coverage (also called fidelity insurance or employee theft insurance) is the most important one for most practices. It covers financial losses caused by dishonest acts committed by your employees—theft of money, forgery or alteration of checks, embezzlement schemes, and computer fraud. This is the coverage that pays when your office manager steals tens of thousands of dollars through fake vendor invoices.

One thing many practice owners don't realize: employee dishonesty coverage is often already included in a Business Owner's Policy (BOP). Check your existing policies, and its limits, before you assume you're unprotected—or that you need to buy standalone coverage.

Commercial Crime Insurance is broader. It extends beyond employees to cover third-party theft—vendors, contractors, outside billing companies. If your outsourced bookkeeper or a vendor with financial system access commits fraud, employee dishonesty coverage may not respond. Commercial crime insurance does. If your practice handles significant cash, processes large electronic transfers, or uses third-party billing services, this coverage deserves serious consideration.

Fidelity Bonds are similar to employee dishonesty coverage but have one important legal dimension: if your practice has a retirement plan, ERISA requires a fidelity bond for anyone who handles plan funds. This is not optional. It is a legal requirement. If your practice offers a 401(k) or similar benefit plan and you don't have a fidelity bond in place, talk to your attorney and insurance agent immediately.

For most small practices, employee dishonesty coverage may be all you need. The other two depend on your specific risk profile. Appendix G provides detailed breakdowns of each coverage type, including what they typically cover, what they exclude, and what to look for in your policy.

What Coverage Costs—and What It's Worth

Coverage is more affordable than most owners expect.

A modest employee dishonesty policy typically costs a few hundred dollars per year. Higher limits cost more—but the increase is often surprisingly small relative to the added protection. The median fraud loss in healthcare exceeds $100,000. A low-limit policy won't make a meaningful dent in a loss of that size. Match your coverage limit to your actual exposure—not your comfort level with premiums.

Consider how many employees handle money, your annual revenues, and how long fraud might go undetected before you'd catch it. Many insurers also offer discounts for documented prevention policies, segregation of duties, and regular audits. Ask specifically about discounts when you call. They may also provide other fraud prevention strategies.

Timing: The Issue Most Owners Get Wrong

Coverage limits matter. But timing matters even more.

Most policies require you to notify the insurer "as soon as practicable" after discovering a loss. That phrase sounds flexible. It isn't. Waiting months—even weeks in some cases—can void your coverage entirely. If fraud is confirmed, notify your insurer within days, not weeks. If you suspect fraud but aren't certain, consult your attorney first, document what you know, and ask whether preliminary notification is warranted.

When you call, be ready with four things: who was involved, what happened, when it started, and an approximate dollar amount. You won't have all the answers yet—that's fine. Notify first, investigate second.

Documentation: What Determines Whether Your Claim Succeeds

Suspicion isn't enough. Insurers require proof.

Start documenting the moment you suspect something. Don't wait until the insurer asks for evidence—by then, records may be harder to reconstruct. What you need:

Proof of the loss —bank statements, canceled checks, altered invoices, system access logs, anything that shows money moved incorrectly.

Proof of the employee's role —transaction records, signatures, access logs that tie the individual to the activity.

Proof you had controls in place —this one surprises owners. Insurers look favorably on practices that had reasonable controls and still experienced fraud. If you can show you required dual signatures, separated duties, and conducted audits—but the employee still found a way around them—your claim is stronger. Controls, that you actually use, prove you weren't negligent.

Keep everything. Organize it as you go. A well-documented claim is a paid claim.

What Insurance Cannot Do

Be clear-eyed about what you're buying.

Insurance cannot prevent fraud from happening. It cannot recover the time you'll spend dealing with the aftermath. It cannot repair damage to staff morale, patient trust, or your reputation in the community. Legal fees and investigation costs are often not fully covered. And no policy eliminates all of the costs—financial, personal, or operational—that fraud leaves behind.

What insurance *can* do is keep your practice financially viable when fraud happens despite your best efforts. That's not a small thing. It's the difference between a painful year and the end of a practice.

Key Principle: Insurance protects your practice when prevention fails—but only if you have adequate coverage, report promptly, and document thoroughly.

Preventative Habits To Start

Review your current policies today. Find out specifically whether you have employee dishonesty coverage, what the limit is, and what the deductible is. If your policy is a BOP, look carefully—coverage may already be there.

Call your insurance agent and ask three specific questions: "If my office manager steals a significant sum through fake vendor checks, am I covered?" "What documentation do I need to file a claim?" "How quickly must I report suspected fraud?" Discuss with them your coverage, so you understand it better.

If you have a retirement plan, confirm with your attorney that you have an ERISA-compliant fidelity bond in place.

Add insurance notification as a required step in your fraud response plan (Chapter 17). It should be automatic, not something you remember later.

Review coverage annually—especially if your practice has grown, you've added financial staff, or your revenues have increased significantly. That should be for the type of coverage, as well as the protection limits.

Notes

Do you have employee dishonesty or crime insurance? Do you know your coverage limits? When did you last review your policy with your agent? Do you have a retirement plan that requires an ERISA fidelity bond?

A Three-Tier Response Plan to Fraud

Responding calmly, legally, and effectively

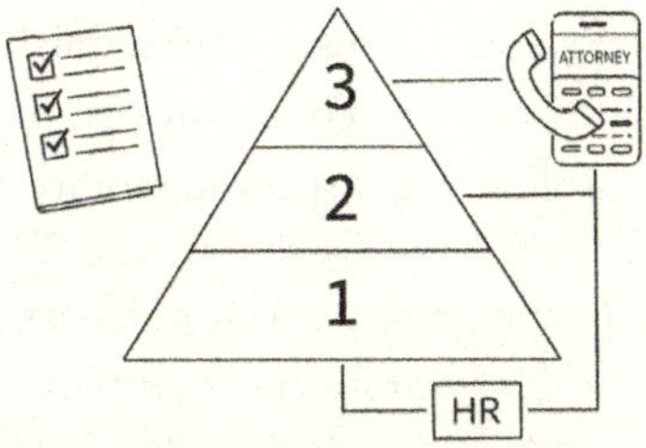

Response Plan

The response was calm. Documented. Predictable.

Everyone knew what would happen next—because it was written down long before it was needed.

The office policy was clear. There was no debate about the outcome. There were no surprises.

That mattered more than the outcome itself.

*****

When fraud is suspected or discovered, it is not the time to guess what to do. The biggest mistake is improvisation in the moment. You need a calm, documented playbook. Your response will be reviewed later - by attorneys, regulators, and insurers - even if the fraud is small. You won't have a second chance to do it correctly.

This content in this chapter is especially valuable to include in your employee handbook and onboarding materials—not because staff must learn how to 'game' it, but because clarity changes behavior. People are less likely to cross the line when the response is written, known, and consistently applied.

Important disclaimer: employment law and reporting requirements vary by state and situation. This is general guidance only. Have your own system established before you need it. When fraud is suspected, involve your practice attorney early and follow state-specific requirements.

Additionally, where appropriate, your business insurance company, that provides your business employee dishonesty and crime coverage, should be included in the notification and remediation process for tier 2 or 3 infractions.

Tier 1: Minor misconduct (corrective action + retention)

Examples: small policy violations, minor misuse of practice resources, first-time issues that appear intentional but limited.

Response: document the facts; meet with the employee (two-person meeting recommended); written warning + remediation plan; restrict access if appropriate; notify counsel for advice on documentation and risk.

Tier 2: Serious misconduct (termination warranted)

Examples: proven theft attempts, falsified time, repeated misconduct after warning, deliberate manipulation of receipts/adjustments.

Response: preserve evidence (reports, logs, receipts); coordinate termination steps with counsel; revoke access immediately (systems, keys, passwords); conduct a brief professional termination meeting; keep internal communications limited to "need-to-know" individuals.

Tier 3: Criminal-level fraud (law enforcement reporting)

Examples: significant theft, forged endorsements, fake vendors, controlled substance diversion, major falsification.

Response: attorney-led plan first; preserve evidence chain; plan insurer notification (employee dishonesty coverage, if applicable); report as advised by counsel. If controlled substances are involved, follow applicable DEA theft/loss reporting rules and processes, where applicable for the type of substance involved (example: DEA Form 106).

Key Principle: A written response plan prevents costly remediation mistakes when fraud is discovered.

Preventative Habits To Start

Write a one-page fraud response checklist now (before you need it) and include it in the handbook.

Identify your attorney and insurer points-of-contact and store them where you can access them quickly.

Keep access revocation steps documented (systems, keys, bank access, vendor portals).

Notes

Do you have a well-defined remediation process that includes actions against employees found to be dishonest? Is it tiered to handle a variety of infraction types? Is it easy to follow under stress?

Appendix A: Sample Fraud Preparedness Checklist

Note: You should review all of your systems for protection. This is only a sample checklist and likely does not contain all elements that you should monitor. Portions of this list are intentionally redundant. Overlap is better than gaps in preventative actions.

Governance & Culture

☐ Written fraud policy in the employee handbook

☐ Non-retaliation reporting policy published

☐ Annual staff acknowledgment

☐ Annual review of insurance needs (coverage types and limits) with agent(s)

Access & Controls

☐ Segregation of financial duties

☐ Restricted systems and bank access

☐ Owner review of high-risk transactions

Cash, Billing & Deposits

☐ Receipts issued for all payments

☐ Daily deposits verified

☐ Refunds and write-offs approved

Payroll

☐ Single timekeeping system

☐ Approval required for edits and overtime

☐ Monthly exception review

Vendors & Inventory

☐ Vendor creation and change is restricted

☐ Invoice → delivery → payment matched

☐ Inventory spot checks performed

Monitoring & Audits

☐ Monthly trend review ("what changed?")

☐ Random audits scheduled (but not announced)

☐ Documentation retained

Reporting & Response

☐ Confidential fraud reporting channel active

☐ Response plan documented

☐ Attorney and insurer contacts identified

Appendix B: Fraud Prevention "Quick Start"

Looking to figure out where to start? Here is a distilled plan that can get you moving on your fraud prevention and detection program. Consider this as your starting line, not your finish line. Prioritize control and action over complexity. A simple control that is done is better than a complex one that is never implemented.

A) Reduce the two big root causes: no controls + unauthorized overrides

Separate duties around money flow

Elements one person should not control: creating vendors, approving invoices, issuing payments and reconciling accounts. In small offices, separation can be "owner reviews, external bookkeeper, different staff roles," not necessarily extra hires.

Owner/physician/admin must do a short monthly "anti-fraud review"

Look for: new vendors, changed remit-to addresses, round-dollar invoices, credits/write-offs trends, refunds, manual checks and unusual adjustments.

Lock down "override" pathways

Require second approval for: vendor adds/changes, ACH changes, refunds/voids and write-offs above a threshold.

B) Focus where risk concentrates: billing and disbursements

Billing controls

Daily/weekly audit sample of claims, adjustments, write-offs, and refunds. Track denial rates and resubmissions by staff user (patterns matter more than totals). Don't forget about billing service companies.

Payments/disbursements controls

Dual authorization on ACH/wires; positive pay on checks if available. Independent review of bank activity and cleared checks/images.

C) Build a detection engine that actually works: tips and monitoring

Simple fraud reporting channel

A dedicated email alias or web form. Make it visible to employees and vendors/customers (because approximately 1/3 of tips are external).

Fraud awareness training (short, recurring)

Not paranoia—pattern recognition: "what looks off," "how to report," and "no retaliation." Keep it simple, but active.

Proactive monitoring

Even basic proactive transaction/data monitoring and reconciliation are associated with meaningfully shorter duration/lower loss versus passive discovery.

D) Don't underestimate concealment (even in "paperless" offices)

Fraud still often involves physical documents (creating/altering them). Practical takeaway: control blank checks, mail handling, vendor statements, and any paper approvals that can be forged.

Appendix C: Sample Handbook Language

Let's get you started with some samples of fraud-related items for your employee handbook. These are SAMPLE POLICY LANGUAGE as an EXAMPLE ONLY, and your own wording for your employee handbook should be formulated by you with consultation with your legal team. Be sure to be (a) accurate in your policy and (b) legally compliant (c) policies should reflect your ACTUAL practice. Having a policy spelled out, but not followed, is a recipe for disaster. Also, remember that these examples are only focused on fraud-related items, not all handbook topics.

1. Financial Integrity Statement

The Practice maintains strict standards for financial integrity. All employees are expected to act honestly, ethically, and in the best interest of the Practice at all times.

2. Segregation of Duties

No employee may independently control all aspects of any financial transaction, including initiation, approval, and reconciliation.

3. Cash and Payment Handling

All payments received must be recorded accurately and receipts issued for every transaction without exception.

4. Refunds and Adjustments

Refunds, write-offs, and adjustments require documentation and approval in accordance with Practice policy. Unauthorized adjustments are prohibited.

5. Payroll Integrity

Falsification of time records, unauthorized overtime, or clocking in/out for another employee constitutes misconduct and may result in disciplinary action, subject to applicable law.

6. Vendor and Purchasing Controls

Only authorized personnel may add, modify, or approve vendors. Employees may not receive direct or indirect personal benefits, monetary or other, from vendor relationships.

7. Use of Practice Property

Practice property, supplies, funds, and equipment are for business use only. Unauthorized use or removal is prohibited.

8. Audits and Reviews

The Practice conducts routine and random audits of financial and operational activities. Cooperation with audits is a condition of employment.

9. Reporting Concerns (Whistleblower)

Employees are encouraged to report suspected misconduct through the designated reporting channel. Reports may be made confidentially.

10. Non-Retaliation

Retaliation against any individual who reports concerns in good faith is strictly prohibited and will result in disciplinary action.

11. Cooperation with Investigations

Employees are expected to cooperate fully with internal or external investigations as needed.

12. Disciplinary Action

Violations of financial policies may result in corrective action, up to and including termination and referral to appropriate authorities, dependent on the nature of the violation, consistent with applicable law.

Appendix D: Fraud Response Checklist

The following fraud-handling checklist and decision framework are provided for illustrative and educational purposes only. Every practice is different, and employment law, reporting obligations, and insurance requirements vary by state and situation. Before adapting or implementing any part of this checklist, you should review and customize it with your attorney and other professional advisors to ensure it aligns with your specific business structure, internal policies, insurance coverage, and applicable laws.

This checklist is designed to help owners and managers respond to suspected or confirmed fraud without panic, improvisation, or legal missteps. It emphasizes process over accusation, documentation over assumption, and control over emotion.

Fraud handling is not a single event. It is a sequence of decisions. How you act early often matters more than what you ultimately find.

PHASE 1: FIRST 48 HOURS AFTER SUSPECTED FRAUD

(Stabilize, preserve, and observe)

Hours 0–6: Immediate Stabilization

☐ Do not confront the employee

☐ Limit discussion to need-to-know basis

☐ Preserve records immediately

☐ Suspend non-essential system changes

☐ Document the trigger event

Hours 6–24: Contain Risk Without Accusation

☐ Tighten controls around the process—not the person

☐ Review recent activity

☐ Secure access if justified

☐ Maintain normal operations

☐ Begin a written timeline

Hours 24–48: Prepare for Formal Review

☐ Consult legal counsel early

☐ Review insurance notification requirements

☐ Evaluate escalation criteria

☐ Preserve evidence integrity

☐ Decide next steps deliberately

PHASE 2: DECISION TREE

Is there a discrepancy? → Is it patterned? → Was there intent? → Does it violate policy or law?

PHASE 3: RESPONSE BY CLASSIFICATION

Administrative Error

Correct, document, monitor. No disciplinary action required.

Policy Violation

Document, coaching, retraining, monitor.

Suspected/Confirmed Fraud

Preserve evidence, consult counsel, notify insurer, restrict access, prepare investigation.

See Chapter 17 for full three-tier response framework.

Appendix E: Sample Audit Schedule

This template provides an example of a structured approach to regular fraud detection through scheduled and random audits. Customize based on your practice size, risk areas, and available resources.

Monthly Tasks

☐ Week 1: Review deposit totals vs. daily reports (select 5 random days from prior month)

☐ Week 2: Analyze refund log – look for patterns, unusual amounts, same patient multiple times

☐ Week 3: Review adjustment/write-off report – require written explanations for increases >10%

☐ Week 4: Spot-check receipt sequence – select random date, verify all numbers present

☐ Throughout month: Owner reviews and approves all refunds >$100 before processing

Quarterly Tasks

☐ Q1 (January-March): Full vendor list review – verify all vendors are legitimate

☐ Q2 (April-June): Inventory spot check – count high-value items, compare to records

☐ Q3 (July-September): Payroll exception analysis – review all time edits, overtime

☐ Q4 (October-December): Banking controls audit – verify signers list current

Annual Tasks

☐ Comprehensive system access review

☐ Policy refresh and staff acknowledgment

☐ External bookkeeper/accountant meeting

☐ Insurance review

Random Tasks (Schedule Throughout Year)

☐ Random receipt sequence verification (6 times per year on different weekdays)

☐ Surprise cash count if applicable (4 times per year)

☐ Mystery patient call or visit (2 times per year)

☐ Random EHR access log review (quarterly)

☐ Unannounced vendor invoice verification (monthly – select 3 invoices)

Implementation Notes

Assign specific owner/manager responsibility for each task. Add tasks to calendar with reminders – treat like patient appointments. Document findings even when "nothing found" – creates audit trail. Adjust frequency based on findings. Don't announce random audits in advance. Start small, then add items. Don't let complexity prevent you from starting.

Appendix F: Exit Procedures Checklist

Proper exit procedures for departing employees—especially those with financial access—are a critical fraud prevention measure. This checklist ensures no access remains active and all property is returned.

Immediate Actions (Day of Termination/Resignation)

System Access Revocation

☐ Disable computer login credentials

☐ Revoke practice management system access

☐ Revoke EHR/EMR access

☐ Disable access to accounting software

☐ Remove from online banking

☐ Revoke vendor portal access

☐ Disable VPN or remote access

☐ Change passwords for shared accounts

Physical Security

☐ Collect office keys

☐ Collect building access cards/fobs

☐ Collect parking passes

☐ Update alarm codes if employee had access

☐ Rekey locks if keys cannot be confirmed returned

Property Return

☐ Collect laptop, tablet, or other computing devices

☐ Collect mobile phone if practice-provided

☐ Collect credit/debit cards

☐ Collect any checks or checkbooks

☐ Collect petty cash if applicable

Within 24-48 Hours

Financial Verification

☐ Review all transactions employee processed in final 30 days

☐ Verify final paycheck amount accurate; Notify payroll service of employee removal from payroll.

☐ Confirm no unauthorized checks issued

☐ Review refund/adjustment log for final week

☐ If employee had vendor access: review recent vendor additions/changes

Communication Management

☐ Set email auto-reply

☐ Forward critical email to designated staff

☐ Update phone system

☐ Notify key vendors/contacts

Within One Week

Banking and Payments

☐ Remove employee as authorized signer on all bank accounts

☐ Update authorized users for ACH/wire transfers

☐ Notify bank of employee departure

☐ Review and update credit card authorized users list

Special Considerations for High-Risk Departures

If termination was for fraud/theft or employee had extensive financial access:

☐ Consider changing all system passwords

☐ Conduct comprehensive audit of transactions from past 6-12 months

☐ Review vendor list for unfamiliar names/addresses

☐ Verify inventory counts

☐ Consult with attorney regarding potential recovery actions

☐ Notify insurance carrier if fraud suspected

Appendix G: Fraud Insurance - A Closer Reference

Use this appendix when you're ready to review an existing policy, shop for new coverage, or discuss with your insurance agent. When meeting, be sure to discuss the scope and coverage limits that your company needs based on current activity. Chapter 16 gives you enough to act. This section gives you enough to decide.

What a Standard Business Owner's Policy (BOP) Typically Covers — and What It Doesn't

A Business Owner's Policy bundles several common coverages into a single policy. Most small practices carry one. Understanding what it includes—and what it leaves out—helps you identify gaps before fraud happens, not after.

A standard BOP typically includes:

General liability (bodily injury and property damage claims from third parties); commercial property coverage (your building, equipment, and contents); business interruption insurance (lost income if operations are disrupted). Some policies include a basic level of employee dishonesty coverage—but this is not universal, and limits are often low.

A standard BOP typically does NOT include:

Adequate employee dishonesty coverage limits for a meaningful fraud loss—if it's included at all, default limits are often low and may fall well short of your actual exposure; commercial crime coverage extending to third-party fraud by vendors, contractors, or outside billing services; cyber liability or data breach coverage (sometimes available as an add-on); ERISA fidelity bond coverage for retirement plan administrators; professional liability or malpractice coverage.

The practical takeaway:

Don't assume your BOP has you covered for internal fraud. Pull out the policy, find the employee dishonesty or crime section, and confirm both that it exists and that the limit is meaningful. If it isn't there—or the limit is too low—talk to your agent about a rider or standalone policy.

Employee Dishonesty Coverage (Fidelity Insurance)

What it is:

Employee dishonesty coverage—also called fidelity coverage or employee theft insurance—protects against financial losses caused by dishonest acts committed by your employees. This is the most relevant coverage for internal fraud and the starting point for most small practices.

What it typically covers:

Theft of money, securities, or property by employees; forgery or alteration of checks; embezzlement schemes, including fake vendor arrangements; computer fraud and funds transfer fraud initiated by an employee; money order and counterfeit currency losses.

What it typically does NOT cover:

Indirect or consequential losses—lost business, reputation damage, or lost productivity; inventory shrinkage from unknown causes (you can't prove who took it); losses discovered more than one year after the employee's termination; dishonest acts by non-employees—vendors, contractors, outside billing services; theft by owners or partners.

Where to find it:

Employee dishonesty coverage is often included in a Business Owner's Policy (BOP). Check your existing BOP before purchasing standalone coverage—you may already have it. If so, verify your coverage levels. It can also be added as a rider to a general liability policy or purchased as standalone coverage.

Coverage limits and costs:

Common limits range from $25,000 to $500,000 or more. Annual premiums are typically modest—and the increase in premium from a low-limit to a higher-limit policy is often surprisingly small. Being underinsured is a common mistake of owners looking to save on premiums. The median fraud loss in healthcare exceeds $100,000. A low-limit policy won't make a meaningful dent in a loss of that size.

Commercial Crime Insurance

What it is:

Commercial crime insurance provides broader protection than employee dishonesty coverage. It extends to third-party crimes and additional fraud scenarios that employee-only policies don't reach.

What it covers beyond employee dishonesty:

Third-party theft by vendors, contractors, or customers; computer fraud and wire transfer fraud (more extensive than most employee dishonesty policies); forgery by non-employees; robbery and burglary; money order and counterfeit instrument fraud from outside parties.

When to consider it:

If your practice handles significant cash, processes large electronic transfers, uses outside billing companies, or relies on outsourced bookkeeping with financial system access, commercial crime insurance closes gaps that employee dishonesty coverage leaves open. Many practices that use third-party billing services are exposed here without realizing it.

If you use an outside billing company, it is important to have them provide you with a summary of their coverages, with limits, and proof of coverage.

Fidelity Bonds

What they are:

Fidelity bonds function similarly to employee dishonesty insurance but are used in specific contexts, most importantly in connection with employee benefit plans.

When they are legally required:

If your practice sponsors a retirement plan—a 401(k), SIMPLE IRA, or similar—ERISA requires a fidelity bond for every person who handles plan funds. This is not optional. The required bond amount is generally 10% of plan assets, with a minimum of $1,000 and a maximum of $500,000 (or $1,000,000 if the plan holds employer securities). If this applies to your practice and you don't have a bond in place, address it immediately with your attorney and insurance agent.

Types of fidelity bonds:

Name schedule bonds cover specifically named individuals. Blanket bonds cover all employees in certain positions—simpler to administer because they automatically cover new hires without requiring policy updates.

Critical Policy Details to Understand Before You Buy — or Before You File

Coverage Amount: Does your limit reflect your actual exposure? Consider annual revenues, number of employees handling money, and how long fraud might go undetected before you'd catch it. Review it annually against growing benefit plan balances to ensure compliance with required coverages.

Deductible: Typically $1,000 to $10,000. Select based on your risk tolerance and other factors.

Discovery Period: Most policies cover losses discovered during the policy period, often with a one-year window after an employee's termination. Losses discovered after that window may not be covered even if the fraud occurred during the policy period. Be fully aware of such limitations.

Proof Requirements: Vague suspicion isn't enough. You must document the loss with specificity—who, what, when, and how much. Start documenting early and be organized.

Common Exclusions: Indirect consequences, inventory shrinkage from unknown causes, theft by owners or partners. Know your exclusions before you assume you're covered.

Notification Timeline: Most policies require notification "as soon as practicable"—typically interpreted as days to a few weeks, not months. Missing this window can void coverage on an otherwise valid claim.

When and How to Notify Your Insurer

If you suspect fraud but aren't certain: Consult your attorney first. Document what you know. Ask your attorney whether preliminary notification to the insurer is warranted at this stage.

If fraud is confirmed: Notify your insurer within days, not weeks. Don't wait until you have the full picture—notify with what you know, then supplement.

For significant losses: Treat insurer notification as mandatory, not optional. This is not the time to handle it internally and report later.

Have ready when you call: Who was involved, what happened, when it likely started, and your best estimate of the dollar amount. Document all calls in your records.

What Strengthens a Claim

The documentation you assemble determines whether your claim succeeds—and how much you recover. Work with your attorney and insurance agent/representative.

Proof of the loss: Bank statements, canceled checks, altered invoices, wire transfer records, system access logs showing unauthorized activity.

Proof of the employee's role: Transaction records tied to the individual, signatures, login records, email or written communications.

Proof you had controls: This is the one that surprises most owners. Insurers look more favorably on practices that had reasonable controls in place and still experienced fraud. Document your policies, your segregation of duties, your audit schedules. They prove you weren't negligent—and a non-negligent claim is a stronger claim. This is also where documentation of your audits is valuable.

Timeline: When the fraud likely started, when you discovered it, what actions you've taken since. Build this chronology from the beginning and update it as you learn more.

What Insurance Cannot Do

Be realistic about the limits of coverage.

Insurance cannot prevent fraud from occurring. It cannot recover the hours you'll spend managing the aftermath—attorney calls, staff meetings, system audits, regulatory questions. It cannot repair damage to staff morale or patient trust. Legal fees and forensic accounting costs are often not fully reimbursed. And even a fully paid claim won't eliminate all the non-financial costs fraud leaves behind.

What coverage *can* do—when combined with strong internal controls—is keep your practice financially viable when fraud happens despite your best efforts. For most practices, that's exactly what it needs to do.

A Note on Premium Costs and Coverage Decisions

The math here generally favors adequate coverage. A modest employee dishonesty policy typically costs a few hundred dollars per year. Higher limits cost more—but the incremental premium increase is often surprisingly small relative to the added protection. Most practices are better served by modest increases in coverage limits than by minimizing premiums.

Ask your agent specifically about discounts. Many insurers reduce premiums for practices that have documented fraud policies, formal segregation of duties, regular audits, and background check procedures. Your prevention program may reduce what you pay for coverage. You can also obtain additional prevention ideas from your insurance company.

Review your coverage annually—particularly when your practice grows, revenues increase, you hire staff with financial access, or your outsourced financial relationships change. Your company's financial status changes from year to year, and your insurance coverages should reflect those changes.

Appendix H: Cyber Fraud and Digital Risks

Most of the fraud discussed in earlier chapters assumes something important: that the risk originates inside your office. That is still true—but it is no longer the whole story. Fraud now enters through your systems—email, banking platforms, remote access, and vendor communications. These are not separate from traditional fraud types. They are extensions of them. In fact, digital tools often make traditional fraud easier, faster, and harder to detect. This appendix focuses on those digital pathways. You will see familiar patterns—opportunity, concealment, and control breakdowns—but applied in ways that are less visible and often more damaging.

This appendix is intended to raise awareness of this specific aspect of fraudulent activity and is not, nor should not, be considered a comprehensive list of possible electronic fraudulent activities. Consider this merely as an "introduction" to such avenues of fraud.

Business Email Compromise (BEC)

Business Email Compromise (BEC) is when an individual engaged in fraud gains access to or spoofs an email account to trick your staff into sending money or sensitive information. This may look like an email from you, a vendor, or a trusted employee. It often includes urgency—"send this now," "payment is overdue," or "new instructions." The criminal is not breaking into your office—they are stepping around it, using your communication system as the entry point.

In many cases, this is not just an external attack. A dishonest employee may use compromised or secondary accounts to create false requests that appear legitimate.

Preventative Habits to Start

Require verbal confirmation (phone call) for any payment request or change—never rely on email alone. Contact the company or individual directly to confirm the request.

Use multi-factor authentication (MFA) on all email accounts, where available.

Train staff to recognize urgency and tone as warning signals—not instructions.

You can also instruct your patients or customer in your standard method of invoicing, so they will not fall victim to invoices from fraudulent sources.

Ensure that employees NEVER click on in-email links or QR codes.

Fake Vendor Payment Changes

This is one of the most common digital fraud schemes. A fraudster sends an email—appearing to come from a vendor—requesting a change in payment details. Bank account numbers are updated, and future payments are diverted.

In some cases, this involves external fraud. In others, an internal employee may initiate or approve these changes without proper verification, using digital systems to conceal the activity.

Preventative Habits To Start

Require independent verification for all vendor payment

changes using known contact information, ideally by phone from a call from YOUR initiation.
Restrict who can change vendor banking details.
Review vendor master file changes monthly.

Phishing and Credential Theft

Phishing is the process of sending fraudulent emails or messages designed to trick someone into revealing passwords or installing malicious software. Once access is obtained, the fraudster can operate inside your systems as if they were a legitimate user.

This dramatically increases the effectiveness of internal fraud. A dishonest employee with additional system access—or the ability to manipulate logs—can conceal activity more effectively.

Preventative Habits to Start
Train staff to NEVER click on unknown links, QR codes or attachments in emails or texts.
Require strong, unique passwords for all systems.
Use endpoint protection and keep systems updated.

ACH and Wire Transfer Fraud

Electronic payments—ACH and wire transfers—are efficient, but they are also high-risk. Once funds are transferred, recovery is difficult or impossible. Fraud in this area often involves altered payment instructions, unauthorized transfers, or manipulation of approval processes.

Digital systems can amplify internal fraud here. A single user with sufficient access can initiate, approve, and conceal transactions within minutes.

Preventative Habits to Start
Require dual approval for ACH and wire transactions.
Set transaction limits and alerts.
Confirm payment instructions verbally before sending funds.
Never transfer funds through unknown links or QR codes in an email or text message.
Never accept payments that are in excess of the amount due, with the request for a refund.

Remote Work Vulnerabilities

Remote access has expanded convenience—but also opportunity. Staff accessing systems from home networks, personal devices, or unsecured environments create additional risk pathways.

This is not just an external issue. Reduced visibility allows internal fraud to occur with less oversight and fewer informal checks.

Preventative Habits to Start
Require secure VPN access for remote work.
Limit access from personal devices.
Monitor login activity and access patterns.

Key Principle: Digital systems increase both the speed and the scale of fraud. Because of the anonymous nature of electronic transactions, all must be confirmed more securely than any other type of transactions where sensitive information, access codes or financial access is provided. Controls must evolve accordingly. Every such transaction should be assumed to be fraudulent until proven legitimate.

General Items

There are common elements that are used in fraudulent actions. One common method is to have individuals (employees, vendors or patients/customers) click on links or QR codes which are sent in emails. This should be prohibited and all electronic sites should only be accessed through trusted URLs supplied by the company directly or through their validated web site.

Ensure that all employees log out of their accounts from their devices on a regular basis, at least daily. Routine change of passwords is standard practice and the use of password managers to help ensure complex passwords are used, and that passwords are not duplicated.

In the era of increasingly sophisticated fraudulent activity AND the rapid development of AI for voice and images, all remote interactions must be viewed with a highly suspicious perspective. When in doubt, assume that fraud is being attempted.

Last, keep all programs up to date and use programs that can help reduce the incidence of fraud, such as VPNs (Virtual Private Networks), Password managers (to help manage individual complex passwords), Anti-virus programs for your computers and utilize services that can help monitor your online footprint and help detect when your personal information is found on the "dark web".

Frequently Asked Questions

Who exactly should do this in a small office?

Even if you only have a small handful of employees, you should implement many of these suggestions. In small practices, the owner's role is often review and verification, not routine execution. But the responsibility of the program remains with the owner or upper management.

How much time will this take?

Implementing these changes can be done one at a time. Keep it manageable to make sure you take action. Once set up, the owner's role should be far easier and faster than the initial phase. Don't let complexity hold you back from starting.

What if I suspect something, but I am wrong?

Strengthening controls is appropriate even when suspicion turns out to be unfounded. And remember to investigate first and take disciplinary actions only AFTER you are sure you have documented nefarious actions.

What do I do first?

Become familiar with the various fraudulent activities in this book. Then start by separating duties, reviewing deposits, and requiring approval for refunds. Then continue on, taking action where you find procedural weakness.

What if I don't have time?

Most of these controls take minutes once they become routine; inconsistency and fraud costs far more time (and money) than prevention.

What if I miss a scheduled review?

Depending on the situation you can reschedule it or wait until the next review, but never abandon the process.

How do I explain these changes without sounding accusatory to my staff?

New controls should be framed as simply implementing standard practice, and not a reaction to any individual's event. Moreover, implementing prior to any event is best for prevention. Most honest employees prefer clear rules and oversight because it helps protect them.

Do I need an outside reviewer or specialist to do this correctly?

Most owners can reduce risk by implementing these suggestions. Outside consultants may be warranted if there is a suspicion for fraudulent activity, to provide an "independent" assessment. But initiation of day-to-day reviews can largely be done by the owner. Just start small and if additional expert help is needed, then add it when necessary.

What if I uncover something small that isn't really "fraud"?

Review each instance of these carefully. Remember that mistakes and some discrepancies can be honest. Those should be documented, corrected and monitored. They are opportunities to help you improve your anti-fraud program.

They are often good sources for employee education and updating of employee policies and procedures.

What should I NOT do if I first suspect fraud?

Do not confront the employee immediately, speculate out loud, or discuss your concerns with other staff. Premature confrontation can destroy evidence, escalate behavior, or expose you to legal risk. The correct first step is to quietly preserve records, tighten controls, and document facts before involving counsel or taking further action.

What should I NOT do to "send a message" to staff?

Fear-based management undermines trust and often discourages honest employees from reporting concerns. Consistent enforcement of written policies is far more effective than dramatic gestures.

What should I NOT ignore because it seems minor?

Do not ignore small, repeated discrepancies—missing receipts, unexplained adjustments, late deposits, or resistance to oversight. These issues often represent early warning signs rather than isolated mistakes. Addressing them early through documentation and process correction prevents escalation.

What should I NOT rely on as my primary fraud safeguard?

Do not rely solely on trust, tenure, software, or external accountants to prevent fraud. Trust is important but not a control. Software and professionals provide tools and reports, but fraud is only detected when someone reviews, understands, and acts on the information. Remember that it is your company and therefore your responsibility.

What should I NOT delay once fraud is confirmed?

Do not delay access revocation, documentation, or legal consultation once fraud is substantiated. Hesitation can increase losses, compromise evidence, and weaken your legal position. A calm, prompt, and documented response protects the practice and limits downstream damage.

What should I NOT do after fraud has been addressed?

Do not return to "business as usual." Failure to correct the underlying control weaknesses that allowed the fraud to occur almost guarantees recurrence. Every confirmed incident should result in process improvement, not just personnel action.

Useful References

ACFE 2024 Report to the Nations on Occupational Fraud and Abuse

https://legacy.acfe.com/report-to-the-nations/2024/

HHS Office of Inspector General — Compliance Guidance

https://oig.hhs.gov/compliance/compliance-guidance/

HHS OIG — Compliance Guidance for Individual and Small Group Physician Practices

https://oig.hhs.gov/documents/compliance-guidance/801/physician.pdf

DEA Diversion Control Division — Theft and Loss Reporting

https://www.deadiversion.usdoj.gov/21cfr_reports/theft/theft-loss.html

DEA — Online Theft/Loss Reporting System (TLR)

https://apps.deadiversion.usdoj.gov/TLR/

DEA — Online Forms and Applications

https://www.deadiversion.usdoj.gov/online_forms_apps.html

21 CFR §1301.74 — DEA Theft and Loss Reporting Regulations

https://www.ecfr.gov/current/title-21/chapter-II/part-1301/subject-group-ECFRa7ff8142033a7a2/section-1301.74

DEA — Theft and Loss FAQ

https://deadiversion.usdoj.gov/faq/theft-loss-faq.html

Note: Many of these references are focused on the reporting of theft of controlled substances, typically from a health-care setting, because of the significant nature of the regulatory elements of such frauds. Many other general references for fraud management may be obtained through online searches.

About the Author

S. Gerard Ruby, MD, MBA is a physician, entrepreneur, patented inventor, and business founder with decades of experience building, leading and managing professional organizations. Trained in both medicine and business, Dr. Ruby has worked at the intersection of clinical practice, executive leadership and institutional governance.

Over the course of his career, he has founded, scaled and exited multiple ventures - experiencing both meaningful successes and instructive failures. Those real-world lessons now form the foundation of his writing and teaching.

His work centers in two primary areas. First, he helps business owners navigate the structural, financial, and governance challenges that emerge as organizations grow. Second, through his personal development work, he guides individuals seeking greater clarity, discipline and intentional growth in both their professional and personal lives.

Dr. Ruby writes for leaders operating where structure, people and power intersect - and for individuals committed to advancing themselves through thoughtful, deliberate action. His books reflect practical insight drawn not from theory alone, but from lived experience.

He lives in the Midwest United States with his wife, and enjoys time with his adult children, grandchildren and dog.

inquiry@rubygrouppublishing.com

Made in United States
Orlando, FL
04 November 2026

90207820R00069